Favourite
TEATIME
RECIPES

GW00706058

Ca

with
of village life by
Trevor Mitchell

Index

Cover pictures *front:* The Village Tearooms *back:* The Village Baker
title page: The Village Post Office

Printed & published by Dorrigo, Manchester, England © Copyright

Chocolate Fudge Cake

These fudge slices are very popular with children. They should be eaten the same day as they are made.

4 oz. hard margarine	2 oz. cocoa powder
10 oz. sugar	Pinch of salt
2 eggs, beaten	1 tablespoon milk
6 oz. self-raising flour	2 drops vanilla essence

Icing sugar for dusting

Set oven to 350°F or Mark 4. Grease and bottom line two 9 inch sandwich tins. Melt the margarine gently in a pan. Put the sugar into a bowl, add the melted margarine and mix well. Beat in the eggs a little at a time with just a little flour at each addition. Add the remainder of the flour, the cocoa powder, salt, the tablespoon of milk and then the vanilla essence. Fold in and mix well together to produce a stiff consistency. Divide the mixture between the tins and smooth the tops. Cook for 20 minutes until springy to the touch. Turn out on to a wire rack. When cool, dust the tops with icing sugar and cut into convenient size segments.

Uplands Biscuits

Vanilla flavoured biscuits, sandwiched together in pairs with raspberry jam, topped with icing and half a glacé cherry.

8 oz. butter, softened	**2 oz. custard powder**
5 oz. sugar	**Pinch of salt**
1 large egg	**Raspberry jam for filling**
10 oz. self-raising flour	**Icing sugar and glacé cherries to decorate**

Set oven to 350°F or Mark 4. Grease baking trays. Beat the butter and sugar together in a bowl until very soft. Beat in the egg, then fold in the flour, custard powder and salt and knead well with floured hands. Roll out on a lightly floured surface to biscuit thickness and cut out with a 2 inch plain cutter. Put on to the baking trays and bake for 10 minutes until pale brown. Transfer to a wire rack and when cold sandwich in pairs with raspberry jam, preferably home-made. Make sufficient glacé icing by mixing icing sugar with just a little water and put a helping on each biscuit. Finally decorate with half a glacé cherry.

Ginger Shortcake

*A traditional shortcake, flavoured with ginger and covered with a layer of
ginger and syrup icing. Serve cut into wedges.*

**8 oz. butter, softened   4 oz. caster sugar   10 oz. flour   2 teaspoons baking powder
2 teaspoons ground ginger**

ICING
2 oz. butter   3 teaspoons golden syrup   4 oz. icing sugar   1 teaspoon ground ginger

Set oven to 325°F or Mark 3. Grease and base line two 9 inch sandwich tins. Beat the butter and sugar together in a bowl until very soft. Sift in the rest of the ingredients and mix well. Knead well with floured hands. Divide between the tins, press down firmly and bake for 40 minutes until golden brown. Turn out on to a wire rack. For the icing, melt the butter and syrup together in a pan, sift in the icing sugar and ground ginger and mix well. Pour equally over each shortbread round and spread out with a warm knife. Cut into wedges while still warm.

Date and Walnut Squares

A succulent date and walnut cake base, topped with a layer of chocolate.

4 oz. soft margarine	1 egg, beaten
5 oz. caster sugar	8 oz. chopped dates
4 oz. self-raising flour	4 oz. chopped walnuts
100 gm. bar plain chocolate	

Set oven to 350°F or Mark 4. Grease and bottom line an approx. 7 x 11 inch shallow tin. Cream the margarine and sugar together in a bowl until light and fluffy. Add the flour, egg, dates and walnuts and mix well. If the mixture seems too stiff add 1 tablespoon of milk. Put into the tin and spread out. Bake for 30 minutes and leave to cool in the tin. Break the chocolate into pieces and melt in a bowl placed over hot water. When the cake is cool, pour the chocolate over, spread out and leave to set. Cut into squares with a sharp knife.

Luscious Lemon Cake

A delicious, intensively lemon flavoured cake, soaked whilst hot with lemon syrup.

**4 oz. soft margarine   6 oz. caster sugar   2 large eggs   6 oz. self-raising flour
Grated rind of 1 lemon   4 tablespoons milk**

SYRUP
3 rounded tablespoons icing sugar   3 tablespoons fresh lemon juice

Set oven to 350°F or Mark 4. Grease and bottom line a 2 lb loaf tin. Cream the margarine and sugar together in a bowl until light and fluffy. Add the eggs, flour, finely grated lemon rind and milk. Mix well to a soft, dropping consistency. Put into the tin, smooth the top and bake for 40 to 45 minutes until firm and a skewer inserted comes out clean. For the syrup, mix the sifted icing sugar and lemon juice together in a bowl and pour over the cake as soon as it comes out of the oven. Leave in the tin until completely cold.

Trevor Mitchell

Picnic Slices

A chocolate base covered with a sweet, coconut and fruit topping; a type of Florentine.

8 oz. plain or milk cooking chocolate	1 egg, beaten
2 oz. butter, softened	4 oz. desiccated coconut
4 oz. caster sugar	2 oz. sultanas

2 oz. glacé cherries, chopped

Set oven to 300°F or Mark 2. Well grease an approx. 7 x 11 inches shallow tin. Break the chocolate into pieces and melt in a bowl placed over hot water. When melted, pour over the bottom of the tin, spread out and leave to set. Cream the butter and sugar together in a bowl until light and fluffy. Add the egg, coconut, sultanas and chopped cherries. Mix well and spread out over the chocolate base in the tin. Bake for about 30 minutes until golden brown. Leave to cool in the tin, then cut into slices with a sharp knife.

Ginger Dessert Cake

A ginger flavoured sponge cake, sandwiched with whipped cream and topped with chocolate icing.

6 oz. soft margarine   5 oz. soft brown sugar   3 eggs   6 oz. self-raising flour
3 rounded teaspoons ground ginger

FILLING and TOPPING
5 fl. oz. whipping cream   A little caster sugar   100 gm. bar plain chocolate
Small knob of butter   2 tablespoons water   8 oz. icing sugar
Crystallised ginger to decorate

Set oven to 350°F or Mark 4. Grease and bottom line two 8 inch sandwich tins. Cream the margarine and sugar together in a bowl until light and fluffy. Add the eggs one at a time and beat each well. Fold in the flour and ginger. Divide between the tins and bake for 25 minutes until springy to the touch. Turn out on to a wire rack. Whip the cream sweetened with a little caster sugar, and use to sandwich the cakes together when cool. For the icing, melt the chocolate and butter, with the water, in a bowl placed over hot water. Sift in the icing sugar and mix well. Pour over the top of the cake and spread out. Decorate with slices of crystallised ginger or, if preferred, with crystallised violets.

Trevor Mitchell

Viennese Tartlets

Dainty little short textured cakes topped with tangy lemon curd. Homemade lemon curd tastes so much nicer than the commercial variety.

8 oz. butter, softened	2 oz. cornflour
2 oz. icing sugar	1 teaspoon vanilla essence
4 oz. plain flour	Icing sugar for dusting

LEMON CURD
Grated zest and juice of ½ large lemon
1½ oz. caster sugar   1 large egg   1 oz. unsalted butter, diced

Set oven to 375°F or Mark 5. Put individual paper cases into patty tins. Cream the butter and icing sugar together in a bowl until really soft. Sift in the flour and cornflour, add the vanilla essence and mix well. Spoon sufficient of the mixture into each paper case to threequarters fill and form a hollow in the centre. Bake for 15 to 20 minutes until pale golden brown in colour. Set aside to cool. When cool, dust each tartlet with icing sugar and put a teaspoonful of homemade lemon curd into the centre of each tartlet. For the lemon curd, combine the lemon zest and sugar in a bowl. In another bowl, beat the egg well with the lemon juice and then pour into the zest and sugar. Add the butter and place the bowl over a pan of hot, not boiling water and cook, very gently, stirring until thick; about 20 minutes. Leave to get cold before using.

Fruit Loaf

An easy to make and fruit filled tea bread.

1 lb. mixed dried fruit
6 oz. Demerara sugar
1 teacup strong tea (no milk)
8 oz. self-raising flour

1 egg
Grated rind of 1 lemon and 1 orange
2 oz. chopped walnuts
1 tablespoon caster sugar

1 oz. butter

Put the fruit, sugar and tea into a bowl and leave to stand overnight, or for as long as possible. Next day, set oven to 325°F or Mark 3. Grease and base line a 2 lb loaf tin. Add the flour, egg and grated rind to the fruit mixture and beat well. Put into the tin and level off. Scatter the chopped walnuts over the top and then the tablespoon of caster sugar. Lastly, dot with small pieces of the butter. Bake for 1 to 1½ hours or until a skewer inserted comes out clean. Leave in the tin for 10 minutes then turn out on to a wire rack. When cold, wrap up in greaseproof paper. Serve the next day, sliced with butter.

Apricot Bread

Apricots with orange rind and juice give this bread an unusual and tangy flavour.

14 oz. plain flour	**½ teaspoon bicarbonate of soda**
6 oz. sugar	**3 oz. raisins or chopped walnuts**
½ teaspoon salt	**6 oz. no-soak apricots, cut up small**
1½ teaspoons baking powder	**1 egg, beaten**

1 oz. butter, melted

Grated rind and juice of 1 orange made up to ⅔ cup with orange juice

Set oven to 350°F or Mark 4. Grease and bottom line a 2 lb loaf tin. Sift all the dry ingredients into a bowl. Add the raisins or nuts and the apricot pieces and mix well. Melt the butter in a pan. Make a well in the mixture, add the egg, the melted butter and the grated rind and orange juice and stir well together. Put into the tin and bake for 50 to 60 minutes or until a skewer inserted comes out clean. Leave in the tin for 10 minutes then turn out on to a wire rack. When cold, wrap up in greaseproof paper and keep for 24 hours before using. This cake may be eaten either sliced plain or with the slices spread with butter.

Ginger Biscuits

Home-made ginger biscuits are always a favourite.

8 oz. self-raising flour	**4 oz. hard margarine**
1 teaspoon bicarbonate of soda	**2 good tablespoons golden syrup**
1 teaspoon ground ginger	**4 oz. caster sugar**

Set oven to 375°F or Mark 5. Grease and flour baking trays. Sift the flour, bicarbonate of soda and ginger into a bowl. Rub in the margarine until the mixture resembles breadcrumbs. Warm the golden syrup in a pan and add to the mixture with the sugar. Mix well to a stiff consistency. With floured hands, roll spoonsful of the mixture into balls the size of a walnut. Place on the baking trays, leaving room to spread out, and flatten each one with a fork. Bake for about 10 minutes. Transfer immediately to a wire rack to cool.

Trevor Mitchell

Almond Slices

A variation of a Bakewell Tart recipe, cut into slices.

8 oz. shortcrust pastry **4 oz. ground almonds**
Apricot jam **2 oz. ground rice**
4 oz. caster sugar **1 whole egg**
4 oz. icing sugar **1 egg white**
Sliced blanched almonds or chopped walnuts for topping

Set oven to 375°F or Mark 5. Well grease an approx. 7 x 11 inches shallow tin. Roll out the pastry on a lightly floured surface to fit and cover the bottom of the tin. Spread a layer of apricot jam over the pastry. Next, mix all the remaining ingredients together in a bowl and spread evenly over the jam layer. Top with sliced almonds or chopped walnuts. Bake for about 20 minutes until pale brown. Slice into fingers in the tin and leave to cool.

Toffee Bars

A sweet, chewy, oaty base covered with a rich chocolate topping.

4 oz. butter, softened   **4 oz. soft brown sugar**   **1 egg yolk**
2 oz. plain flour   **2 oz. porridge oats**

TOPPING
3 oz. plain cooking chocolate   **1 oz. butter**   **2 oz. finely chopped walnuts**

Set oven to 375°F or Mark 5. Well grease an approx. 7 x 11 inches shallow tin. In a bowl, beat together the butter, sugar and egg yolk until smooth. Mix in the flour and oats. Put the mixture into the tin, spread out evenly and press down. Bake for 15 to 20 minutes until golden brown. Cool slightly in the tin. Meanwhile, break up the chocolate into a bowl with the butter and melt over hot water. Spread the chocolate over the mixture in the tin and cover with chopped walnuts. Cut into bars with a sharp knife while still warm, but leave in the tin to get completely cold before turning out.

Yorkshire Tea Cakes

Flat, round cakes made with yeast dough and flavoured with currants.
Best served toasted with plenty of butter.

¾ pt lukewarm milk	4 oz. lard
1 oz. fresh yeast	4 oz. sugar
2 lb. strong white flour	4 oz. currants
2 teaspoons salt	1 egg, beaten

Grease and flour baking trays. Blend the yeast with 1 teaspoon of the sugar and dissolve in the milk. Sift the flour and salt into a bowl and rub in the lard. Stir in the sugar and currants. Make a well, add the milk/yeast mixture and the beaten egg and mix to a soft dough. Knead on a floured surface for about ten minutes, place in a clean bowl, cover and leave in a warm place until doubled in size. Knead again gently, then divide into pieces that will form into 4 inch rounds. Place on the baking trays, prick with a fork, cover and leave for about 30 minutes to rise again. Meanwhile, set oven to 425°F or Mark 7. When the tea cakes have proved, bake for about 15 to 20 minutes until brown. Transfer to a wire rack to cool.

Rich Seed Cake

A moist, Madeira-type cake flavoured with caraway seeds and spices; an old fashioned tea time favourite, which keeps well and improves in flavour with keeping.

8 oz. butter, softened **8 oz. self-raising flour**
8 oz. sugar **1 oz. caraway seeds**
4 eggs, separated **½ teaspoon ground nutmeg**
½ teaspoon ground cinnamon

Set oven to 350°F or Mark 4. Grease and line a 7 inch round cake tin. Cream the butter and sugar together in a bowl until light and fluffy. Beat the egg whites stiffly and fold in, then work in the beaten egg yolks. Gradually fold in the flour, caraway seeds and spices. Put into the tin and bake for 1 hour or until a skewer inserted comes out clean. Leave in the tin for 5 minutes then turn out on to a wire rack to cool.

Sultana and Cherry Cake

A succulent fruit cake bursting with sultanas and glacé cherries.

4 oz. glacé cherries	4 oz. caster sugar
12 oz. sultanas	3 large eggs, beaten
4 oz. butter, softened	6 oz. plain flour

Pinch of salt

Set oven to 325°F or Mark 3. Grease and base line a 2 lb loaf tin. Wash the cherries, pat dry on kitchen paper, cut in half and dredge in flour with the sultanas. Cream the butter and sugar together in a bowl until light and fluffy. Beat in the eggs a little at a time, with a little flour with each addition. Fold in the remaining flour with the salt. Add the cherries and sultanas and mix well together to distribute the fruit evenly. Put into the tin and bake for 1½ to 1¾ hours or until a skewer inserted comes out clean. Leave in the tin to cool.

Orange and Almond Cake

A light and delicious orange flavoured cake which does not rise very much.

2 oz. fine breadcrumbs   **Juice of 3 oranges**
4 oz. ground almonds   **2 eggs, separated**
Grated rind of 1 orange   **4 oz. caster sugar**
5 fl. oz. whipping cream for topping

Set oven to 350°F or Mark 4. Grease and line a 9 inch round cake tin. In a bowl, combine together the breadcrumbs, ground almonds and orange rind and juice. Beat together the egg yolks and sugar and stir into the breadcrumbs/orange mixture. Beat the egg whites stiffly and fold in. Put into the tin and bake for 30 minutes or until a skewer inserted comes out clean. Leave to cool in the tin before turning out. When cold, whip the cream and spread over the top of the cake and decorate as preferred.

Coconut Meringue Slices

A sweet pastry base with a coconut meringue topping.

3 oz. soft margarine   4 oz. sugar   6 oz. self-raising flour   2 tablespoons milk
2 egg yolks   ½ teaspoon salt

TOPPING
2 stiffly beaten egg whites   4 oz. sugar   2 oz. desiccated coconut
1 oz. chopped mixed nuts   1 oz. glacé cherries, chopped

Set oven to 350°F or Mark 4. Grease and base line an approx. 7 x 11 inches shallow tin. Cream the margarine and sugar together in a bowl until light and fluffy. Then add the rest of the ingredients and mix well. Put into the tin, spread out and press down firmly. For the topping, first beat the egg whites until stiff. Then mix all the ingredients together in a bowl and spread evenly over the mixture in the tin. Bake for about 20 minutes until pale brown. Cut into slices in the tin and allow to cool.

Spicy Layer Cake

An unusual, spicy sponge cake made with evaporated milk and filled with lemon butter icing.

6 oz. plain flour   1 level teaspoon baking powder   ½ level teaspoon salt
½ level teaspoon bicarbonate of soda   ½ level teaspoon ground mixed spice
½ level teaspoon ground cinnamon
4 oz. soft margarine   5 oz. granulated sugar   3 oz. soft brown sugar
2 eggs, beaten   170 gm. tin evaporated milk

FILLING and TOPPING
2 oz. softened butter   4 oz. sifted icing sugar   Juice of ½ lemon
Icing sugar for dusting

Set oven to 350°F or Mark 4. Grease and base line two 9 inch sandwich tins. Sift together all the dry ingredients twice. Cream the margarine and sugars together in a bowl until light and fluffy. Add the eggs, all the dry ingredients and the evaporated milk and mix well. Divide between the tins and bake for 30 minutes until light brown and springy to the touch. Turn out on to a wire rack to cool. For the filling, cream together in a bowl the butter, sugar and lemon juice and use to sandwich the cakes together. Dust the top with icing sugar.

Rich Almond Cake

A rich textured, well flavoured cake.

4 oz. butter, softened	3 oz. ground almonds
5 oz. caster sugar	1½ oz. plain flour
3 eggs	2 drops almond essence

Icing sugar for dusting

Set oven to 350°F or Mark 4. Grease and line a 7 inch round cake tin. Put the softened butter into a bowl and add the sugar gradually, beating well. Add the eggs one at a time, with one third of the ground almonds with each egg and mix well. Fold in the flour and almond essence. Put into the tin and bake for 40 to 45 minutes or until a skewer inserted comes out clean. Leave in the tin for 5 minutes then turn out on to a wire rack. When cool dust the top with icing sugar.

Buttermilk Bread

A soft, light textured bread which needs to be eaten the same day as it is made.

1 lb. plain flour	1 teaspoon bicarbonate of soda
1 teaspoon cream of tartar	1 teaspoon salt

About 1 breakfast cup buttermilk
or use 1 dessertspoon vinegar made up to a cupful with fresh milk

Set oven to 425°F or Mark 7. Grease and flour a baking tray. Sift the flour and all the other dry ingredients together into a bowl. Mix in just enough buttermilk to make a dough which adheres together in a ball. Divide the dough into two pieces, shape into rounds and place on the baking tray. Mark the top of each loaf with a sharp knife and bake for 20 minutes until pale brown. The loaves will be cooked when the bottoms sound hollow when tapped. Transfer to a wire rack to cool. Serve sliced and buttered.

Coconut Cake

A lemon and almond flavoured base, spread with jam and finished with a coconut topping.

4 oz. soft margarine   3 oz. soft brown sugar   Grated rind of 1 lemon
2 drops almond essence   1 egg, beaten   12 oz. plain flour   Apricot jam

TOPPING
1 egg, beaten   3 oz. soft brown sugar   8 oz. desiccated coconut

Set oven to 350°F or Mark 4. Well grease an approx. 7 x 11 inches shallow tin. Cream the margarine and sugar together in a bowl until light and fluffy. Add the lemon rind, almond essence and egg and mix well together. Add the flour and mix well. Put into the tin, spread out and press down. Spread with a layer of apricot jam. For the topping, mix together in a bowl the egg, sugar and coconut and spread evenly over the jam filling. Bake for 20 to 30 minutes until firm. Leave in the tin to cool before cutting into slices. Store in an airtight tin.

Grasmere Gingerbread

A famous recipe from Wordsworth's home village in the Lake District.

9 oz. wholemeal flour

3 oz. porridge oats

¾ teaspoon bicarbonate of soda

1½ teaspoons cream of tartar

3 teaspoons ground ginger

9 oz. hard margarine

9 oz. soft brown sugar

Set oven to 325°F or Mark 3. Well grease and base line an approx. 14 x 9 inches shallow tin. Put the flour, oats, bicarbonate of soda, cream of tartar and ground ginger into a bowl. Cut the margarine into small pieces and rub in until the mixture resembles breadcrumbs. Stir in the sugar. Put into the tin, spread out and press down firmly with the back of a floured fork. Bake for 20 to 30 minutes until pale brown. Cut into squares while warm and leave in the tin until completely cold. Keeps well in an airtight tin.

THE
VILLAGE
BAKERY

BREAD
CAKES
PASTRIES

HOMEMADE
SCONES
&
CAKES

FRESH
PIES &
PASTRIES

Dales Bakers

Trevor Mitchell

Caramel Shortbread

A caramel toffee filling sandwiched between chocolate and shortbread.
Very popular with children and adults alike!

4 oz. butter, softened   2 oz. sugar   6 oz. self-raising flour   Pinch of salt

TOPPING
4 oz. caster sugar   4 oz. butter   2 tablespoons golden syrup
218 gm. tin condensed milk   100 gm. bar plain or milk chocolate

Set oven to 325°F or Mark 3. Well grease and base line an approx. 11 x 7 inches shallow tin. Cream the butter and sugar together in a bowl until light and fluffy. Stir in the flour and salt and knead well. Put into the tin, spread out and press down evenly with the fingers. Bake for 30 minutes until pale brown. Leave in the tin to cool. Meanwhile, for the topping, put all the ingredients, except the chocolate, into a pan. Bring to the boil and continue boiling for 5 minutes or more, stirring continuously until the mixture thickens and turns pale caramel brown. When ready, pour over the cooked shortbread and spread out. When set, melt the chocolate in a bowl set over hot water, pour over the caramel and spread out. When the chocolate has set, cut into squares with a sharp knife dipped in hot water.

Almond Biscuits or Tuiles

These dainty biscuits go well with coffee or with fresh fruit salad.

3 oz. butter, softened　　**2 oz. plain flour**
3 oz. caster sugar　　**Pinch of salt**
3 oz. blanched almonds, shredded

Set oven to 375°F or Mark 5. Well grease and flour a baking tray. Cream the butter and sugar together in a bowl until light and fluffy. Sift in the flour and salt, add the shredded almonds and mix together. Put teaspoonsful of the mixture on to the baking tray, leaving plenty of room for them to spread. Bake for 6 to 8 minutes. Allow to cool for a few seconds, then remove with a sharp knife and lay over a rolling pin to curl around until set. Bake in batches as convenient.

Trevor Mitchell

Butter Drops

These crisp, buttery biscuits are delicious with a cup of coffee.

4 oz. butter	**2 large eggs, beaten**
4 oz. caster sugar	**5 oz. plain flour**
½ level teaspoon baking powder	

Set oven to 325°F or Mark 3. Grease and flour baking trays. Melt the butter slowly in a pan until it turns pale brown. Remove from the heat and leave to cool for 10 minutes. Next, beat in the sugar and eggs. Sift the flour and baking powder into the pan and stir. Put teaspoonsful of the mixture on to the baking trays, leaving plenty of room for them to spread during cooking. Bake for about 20 minutes, when they should be golden brown around the edges. Transfer immediately to a wire rack to cool.

Rice Loaf

This is a popular recipe for people who like a plain cake.

6 oz. butter, softened   1 teaspoon baking powder
6 oz. caster sugar   Pinch of salt
3 eggs, beaten   4 oz. ground rice
4 oz. plain flour   2 oz. ground almonds
1 tablespoon warm water

Set oven to 350°F or Mark 4. Grease and bottom line a 2 lb loaf tin. Cream the butter and sugar together in a bowl until light and fluffy. Add the eggs and dry ingredients gradually, mixing between each addition. Finally, add the warm water and stir the mixture until smooth. Put into the tin and bake for about 1 hour until golden brown and a skewer inserted comes out clean. Leave in the tin for 15 minutes then turn out on to a wire rack to cool.

Banana Nut Bread

*A moist tea bread recipe containing mashed bananas and chopped walnuts.
Useful for using up bananas that are getting over ripe.*

4 oz. butter, softened	1 teaspoon bicarbonate soda
6 oz. caster sugar	2 very ripe bananas
2 eggs, well beaten	12 oz. self-raising flour
3 tablespoons sour milk	1 teaspoon vanilla essence
6 oz. chopped walnuts	

Set oven to 350°F or Mark 4. Grease and bottom line a 2 lb loaf tin. Cream the butter and sugar together in a bowl until light and fluffy, then mix in the eggs. Mix the bicarbonate of soda with the sour milk. Mash the bananas, add them to the mixture with the flour and milk and mix well. Stir in the vanilla essence and the nuts. Put into the tin and bake for 40 to 45 minutes until firm and a skewer inserted comes out clean. Leave in the tin for 15 minutes then turn out on to a wire rack. When cold, serve sliced and buttered.

Coffee Cake

*A traditional coffee sponge, sandwiched and topped with coffee butter icing
and decorated with chopped walnuts.*

**6 oz. soft margarine   6 oz. sugar   2 heaped teaspoons instant coffee granules
1 tablespoon hot water   3 eggs, beaten   7 oz. self-raising flour
Pinch of salt   1 teaspoon baking powder**

ICING and TOPPING
**4 oz. butter, softened   8 oz. icing sugar   1 tablespoon coffee essence
Chopped walnuts to decorate**

Set oven to 375°F or Mark 5. Grease and base line two 8 inch sandwich tins. Cream the margarine and sugar together in a bowl until light and fluffy. Dissolve the coffee granules in the hot water. Beat in the eggs gradually, with a little flour with each addition. Sieve in the remaining flour with the salt and baking powder and fold in. Add the coffee mixture and mix well. Divide between the tins and bake for about 20 minutes until springy to the touch. Turn out on to a wire rack to cool. For the icing, mix the butter, sugar and coffee essence together in a bowl and blend well. Use to sandwich the cakes together and to cover the top. Finally, decorate with chopped walnuts.

Trevor Mitchell

Coconut Cookies

A dainty, melt-in-the-mouth tea time treat.

2 egg whites   **6 oz. desiccated coconut**
4 oz. caster sugar   **Rice paper**

Set oven to 325°F or Mark 3. Grease a baking sheet and cover with rice paper. Whisk the egg whites in a bowl until very stiff. Then, gradually fold in the sugar and the coconut. Drop dessertspoonsful of the mixture on to the rice paper, allowing some space for spreading. Bake for 15 minutes until beginning to brown on top. Allow to cool on the baking sheet before removal and separation.

Date and Cherry Cake

A fruity tea bread to be eaten sliced and buttered.

2 oz. hard margarine   12 oz. self-raising flour   ½ teaspoon salt
½ teaspoon bicarbonate of soda   ½ pt boiling water
4 oz. glacé cherries   4 oz. dates   12 oz. sugar
1 egg   1 teaspoon vanilla essence

Set oven to 350°F or Mark 4. Grease and line a 7 inch square cake tin. In a bowl, rub the margarine into the flour with the salt. In another bowl, dissolve the bicarbonate of soda in the boiling water. Chop the cherries and dates into convenient size pieces. Put all the dry ingredients, the egg, vanilla essence and the hot water into the flour mixture and mix well. Put into the tin and bake for 1½ hours or until a skewer inserted comes out clean. Leave in the tin for 15 minutes to cool, then turn out on to a wire rack. When cold, serve sliced and buttered.

Russian Tipsy Cake

*A fatless, marbled sponge cake, moistened with fruit juice and rum and
sandwiched and topped with whipped cream.*

**1 oz. plain cooking chocolate   3 tablespoons boiling water
3 eggs   4½ oz. caster sugar   2¼ oz. plain flour   Pinch of salt
1 extra tablespoon plain flour**

FILLING and TOPPING
**2 tablespoons fruit juice (to choice)   2 tablespoons rum   ½ pt. double cream
Chocolate drops for decoration**

Set oven to 375°F or Mark 5. Grease a 9 inch round cake tin and dust with caster
sugar and flour mixed. Melt the chocolate in the boiling water. In a bowl, whisk the
eggs and sugar together, preferably with an electric mixer, until thick. Fold in the
flour and salt. Put half the mixture into another bowl. Stir the melted chocolate into
one bowl and the extra flour into the other. Put alternate spoonsful of the mixtures
into the tin to give a marbled effect. Bake for 30 to 40 minutes or until a skewer
inserted comes out clean. Leave in the tin to cool then turn out and split in half. Mix
the fruit juice and rum together and spoon over the two cut halves. Use the double
cream (whipped if not thick enough) to sandwich the two halves together. Decorate
the top with whirls of cream and chocolate drops.

Farmhouse Sponge

A plain, fatless sponge filled with generous layers of raspberry jam and whipped cream.

3 large eggs, separated   5 oz. caster sugar   4 oz. self-raising flour   Pinch of salt

FILLING and TOPPING
Raspberry jam   5 fl.oz. whipping cream   Icing sugar for dusting

Set oven to 375°F or Mark 5. Grease and flour two 9 inch sandwich tins. First, slightly warm the bowl in the oven or in hot water. Whisk the egg whites until stiff. Add the sugar and egg yolks and whisk until thick and creamy. Fold in the flour and salt with a metal spoon. Divide between the tins and put straight into the oven. Bake for 20 to 30 minutes until light brown and springy to the touch. Turn out on to a wire rack to cool. When cold, sandwich thickly with raspberry jam and whipped cream. Dust the top with icing sugar.

Currant Pasties

Puff or shortcrust pastry squares sandwiched with a rum butter and currant filling.

8 oz. puff or shortcrust pastry
1½ oz. butter   1½ oz. soft brown sugar
8 oz. currants   3-4 drops lemon juice   1 tablespoon rum
Caster sugar for sprinkling

Set oven to 450°F or Mark 8. Grease and flour a baking tray. Roll out the pastry thinly on a lightly floured surface to a large square, about 14 x 14 inches. Cut in half and put one half on the baking tray. Melt the butter and sugar together gently in a pan, remove from the heat, add the rest of the ingredients and mix well. Put the filling on the pastry on the baking tray and spread out evenly. Brush the pastry edges with water, place the other pastry half on top and seal the edges well. Mark into squares with a sharp knife and make a few airholes in each one with a fork. Brush the top lightly with milk and sprinkle with caster sugar. Bake for 20 to 25 minutes until golden brown. Leave on the tray to cool and cut up when cold.

METRIC CONVERSIONS

The weights, measures and oven temperatures used in the preceding recipes can be easily converted to their metric equivalents. The conversions listed below are only approximate, having been rounded up or down as may be appropriate.

Weights

Avoirdupois	Metric
1 oz.	just under 30 grams
4 oz. (¼ lb.)	app. 115 grams
8 oz. (½ lb.)	app. 230 grams
1 lb.	454 grams

Liquid Measures

Imperial	Metric
1 tablespoon (liquid only)	20 millilitres
1 fl. oz.	app. 30 millilitres
1 gill (¼ pt.)	app. 145 millilitres
½ pt.	app. 285 millilitres
1 pt.	app. 570 millilitres
1 qt.	app. 1.140 litres

Oven Temperatures

	°Fahrenheit	Gas Mark	°Celsius
Slow	300	2	150
	325	3	170
Moderate	350	4	180
	375	5	190
	400	6	200
Hot	425	7	220
	450	8	230
	475	9	240

Flour as specified in these recipes refers to plain flour unless otherwise described.